# *The* Noodle
## COOKBOOK

## The Family Circle® Promise of Success

Welcome to the world of Confident Cooking, created for you in the
**Family Circle® Test Kitchen,** where recipes are double-tested by our team
of home economists to achieve a high standard of success.

**MURDOCH BOOKS**®

*Sydney • London • Vancouver • New York*

# KNOW YOUR NOODLES

Noodles have been relished since ancient times, and their popularity has now become wide indeed. And rightly so: fresh or dried, they make for meals that are as versatile as they are tasty and quick.

An increasing range of noodles are now being stocked on supermarket shelves, but if you venture into an Asian grocery store, you'll be greeted with noodles of every imaginable shape, width, colour and flavour—and being so inexpensive, you won't need to resist the temptation to stock up!

Here are some of the noodles you'll be most likely to find. See pages 62–63 for a glossary of other common noodle-related ingredients.

### EGG NOODLES
Ranging from very thin to quite thick, egg noodles are made from egg and wheat flour.

Fresh egg noodles are traditional to Chinese chow mein and Japanese ramen dishes, but are now used widely. Fresh egg noodles need to be refrigerated until ready to use, and all egg noodles, fresh or dried, should be cooked in boiling water before use.

### UDON NOODLES
These white Japanese wheat flour noodles vary in thickness and shape and are cooked in boiling water before use. They are especially lovely in the fresh form.

### SOMEN NOODLES
Similar to udon, these fine, round Japanese wheat flour noodles are usually sold dried.

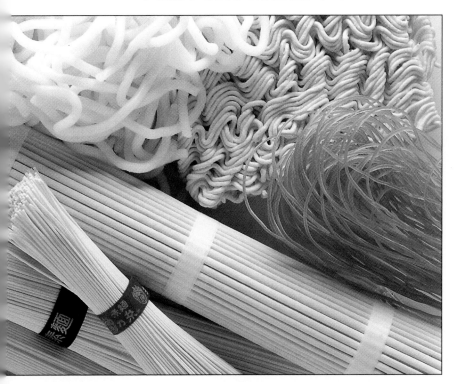

**RICE SPAGHETTI**
Resembling cooked spaghetti, these fresh, round, white noodles are also known as laksa noodles. If not readily available, substitute dried rice vermicelli.

**INSTANT NOODLES**
Supermarkets stock many brands of dried instant noodles. They are made from wheat flour and are very quick to prepare.

**DRIED POTATO NOODLES**
Also known as Korean vermicelli, these long,

fine, greenish-brown translucent noodles need to be cooked in boiling water, then rinsed and drained well before using. On cooking, they become plump and gelatinous, but if overcooked they will break down and become sticky.

1 *Fresh thick egg noodles*
2 *Dried thick egg noodles*
3 *Fresh thin egg noodles*
4 *Dried thin egg noodles*
5 *Fresh udon noodles*
6 *Dried udon noodles*
7 *Dried somen noodles*
8 *Fresh rice spaghetti*
9 *Instant noodles*
10 *Dried potato noodles*

**FRESH RICE NOODLES**
Available thick or thin, these white rice noodles are steamed and lightly oiled before packing, and so are sold ready to use. If refrigerated they will become hard, but soften on heating.

**FRESH RICE NOODLE ROLLS**
These noodles are sold in a sheet or roll, which can be cut to a desired width. It is important that they are very fresh, otherwise they will be difficult to unroll and may even crack. They need to be brought to room temperature before being handled.

**DRIED RICE STICKS**
Resembling fettuccine, these translucent, flat dried noodles are often used in stir-fries, and also in soups and salads. They are packaged in bundles. Soak in warm water before using.

**DRIED RICE VERMICELLI**
Packaged in blocks, these thin, translucent, whitish noodles need to be soaked in boiling water (or boiled until tender) and well drained before use. When deep-fried, vermicelli noodles expand and are often used as a garnish.

**SOBA NOODLES**
These noodles are a northern Japanese speciality made from buckwheat and/or wheat flour. They are eaten hot or cold, and are available both fresh and dried, in various colours and flavours.

**CELLOPHANE NOODLES**
Also known as mung bean vermicelli or glass noodles, these flat or

thread-like, translucent noodles are made from mung beans and sold packaged in blocks. They are very hard to cut, but soften when cooked in boiling water. A little goes a long way. When fried in hot oil, either straight from the packet or after being soaked and drained, they puff up.

**HOKKIEN NOODLES**
These popular thick, yellow noodles are made from egg and wheat flour and are sold ready to use, being precooked and lightly oiled. Simply stir-fry the noodles, or add them to soups or salads. Hokkien noodles are used in many Asian cuisines, including those of Malaysia and Singapore. Keep the noodles refrigerated. Asian brands are of a higher quality.

1 *Fresh thick rice noodles*
2 *Fresh rice spaghetti*
3 *Fresh rice noodle rolls*
4 *Dried rice sticks*
5 *Dried rice vermicelli*
6 *Dried soba noodles*
7 *Dried green tea soba noodles*
8 *Cellophane noodles*
9 *Hokkien noodles*

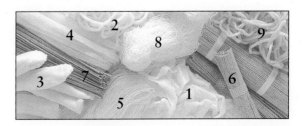

# Noodles

Hungry for a satisfying meal or snack? The humble noodle never fails to deliver. From slurpy soups to savoury stir-fries, noodles are thirsty for your favourite flavours.

## Prawn and Noodle Soup

*Preparation time:*
  20 minutes
*Total cooking time:*
  30 minutes
*Serves 6*

500 g (1 lb) raw prawns
1–2 tablespoons oil
1 stem lemon grass,
  chopped
2 cloves garlic,
  chopped
2 small red chillies,
  sliced in half
2 fresh kaffir lime leaves
1 lime, quartered, and
  extra to garnish
4 spring onions, sliced
  on the diagonal
500 g (1 lb) dried udon
  noodles
2 tablespoons soy sauce
100 g (3¼ oz) shiitake
  mushrooms, sliced in
  half
¼ cup (7 g/¼ oz) fresh
  coriander leaves
1 bunch baby bok choy,
  washed and trimmed,
  leaves separated

**1.** Peel and devein the prawns, reserving the heads and shells. Heat the oil in a large pan, add the prawn heads and shells and cook over high heat until pink.
**2.** Add the lemon grass, garlic, red chillies, lime leaves, lime quarters, half the spring onions and 2 litres water. Bring to the boil, reduce the heat and simmer for 20 minutes. Strain finely and discard the solids.
**3.** Cook the noodles in plenty of boiling salted water for 5 minutes, or until tender. Drain well.
**4.** Bring the stock to the boil. Add the soy sauce and prawns and cook until the prawns turn pink. Add the rest of the ingredients; season to taste. Transfer the noodles to soup bowls, ladle the soup over and serve with a lime wedge.

NUTRITION PER SERVE
*Protein 30 g; Fat 7 g;
Carbohydrate 70 g; Dietary
Fibre 1 g; Cholesterol
125 mg; 1865 kJ (445 cal)*

*Prawn and Noodle Soup*

## Spicy Egg Noodles with BBQ Pork

*Preparation time:*
  15 minutes
*Total cooking time:*
  10 minutes
*Serves 4*

$1/2$ cup (125 g/4 oz)
  crunchy peanut butter
3 tablespoons oil
2 teaspoons sesame oil
2 tablespoons soy sauce
2 teaspoons garam
  masala
2 cloves garlic, crushed
1 tablespoon sweet
  chilli sauce
250 g (8 oz) dried egg
  noodles (not too fine)
250 g (8 oz) barbecued
  pork, finely sliced
120 g (4 oz) broccoli
  florets
2 spring onions, sliced

**1.** Combine the peanut butter, oils, soy sauce, garam masala, garlic and sweet chilli sauce. Mix well and set aside.
**2.** Boil the noodles until tender; drain well and set aside. Add the sauce mixture to the same hot pan to soften. Toss in the pork and noodles; cover and keep warm.
**3.** Cook the broccoli in salted boiling water for 3 minutes. Drain well and add to the noodles. Toss over gentle heat.

**4.** Garnish with spring onion and serve at once.

NUTRITION PER SERVE
*Protein 30 g; Fat 40 g;
Carbohydrate 50 g; Dietary
Fibre 8 g; Cholesterol
50 mg; 2825 kJ (670 cal)*

## Egg Spring Rolls with Sesame Sauce

*Preparation time:*
  35 minutes
*Total cooking time:*
  30–35 minutes
*Makes 12*

**Sesame Sauce**
2 tablespoons fish sauce
4 tablespoons lime juice
3 teaspoons sesame oil
1 tablespoon toasted
  sesame seeds

8 eggs
50 g ($1^3/4$ oz) cellophane
  noodles
1 tablespoon oil
1 clove garlic, crushed
2 teaspoons grated
  fresh ginger
150 g (5 oz) pork mince
150 g (5 oz) raw peeled
  prawns, deveined and
  chopped
1 carrot, grated
2 spring onions, sliced
50 g ($1^3/4$ oz) shredded
  Chinese cabbage
3 tablespoons sweet
  chilli sauce
2 tablespoons fresh
  coriander leaves

**1.** To make the sesame sauce, combine all the sauce ingredients. Mix well and set aside.
**2.** Whisk together the eggs and 4 tablespoons water. Heat a lightly oiled omelette pan and pour in 2 tablespoons of the egg mixture, swirling gently to cover the base of the pan. Cook over low heat for 1–2 minutes, then turn and cook for 1 minute. Transfer to a plate and repeat with the rest of the mixture.
**3.** Place the noodles in a heatproof bowl; cover with boiling water for 3–4 minutes, or until soft. Drain well, then cut into shorter lengths with a pair of scissors.
**4.** Heat the oil in a wok, add the garlic and ginger and cook over high heat for 30 seconds. Add the mince and prawns and cook for 4–5 minutes, breaking up any lumps. Add all the ingredients except the omelettes and toss well.
**5.** Spoon 2 tablespoons of the mixture onto the middle of an omelette. Fold the edges into the centre, then røll up tightly. Repeat with the remaining ingredients and serve with the sesame sauce.

NUTRITION PER ROLL
*Protein 10 g; Fat 8 g;
Carbohydrate 4 g; Dietary
Fibre 1 g; Cholesterol
145 mg; 550 kJ (130 cal)*

---

*Spicy Egg Noodles with BBQ Pork (top)
and Egg Spring Rolls with Sesame Sauce*

# Singapore Noodles

*Preparation time:*
*35 minutes +*
*5 minutes soaking*
*Total cooking time:*
*15 minutes*
*Serves 2–4*

*300 g (10 oz) dried*
*rice vermicelli*
*2 tablespoons oil*
*2 cloves garlic, finely*
*chopped*
*350 g (11¹/4 oz) pork*
*loin, cut into strips*
*300 g (10 oz) peeled*
*raw prawns, deveined*
*1 large onion, cut into*
*thin wedges*
*1–2 tablespoons curry*
*powder*
*155 g (5 oz) green*
*beans, cut into short*
*lengths*
*1 large carrot, sliced*
*1 teaspoon sugar*
*1 teaspoon salt*
*1 tablespoon soy sauce*
*200 g (6¹/2 oz) bean*
*sprouts, scraggly ends*
*removed*
*1 spring onion, cut into*
*fine strips, to garnish*

1. Soak the vermicelli in boiling water for about 5 minutes, or until soft. Drain well.
2. Heat half the oil in a wok over high heat and add the garlic, pork and prawns. Stir-fry for 2 minutes, or until the mixture is just cooked. Remove from the wok and set aside.

3. Reduce the heat to medium. Add the rest of the oil and stir-fry the onion and curry powder for 2–3 minutes. Add the beans, carrot, sugar and salt, sprinkle with a little water and stir-fry for 2 minutes.
4. Toss the vermicelli and soy sauce through. Add the bean sprouts, prawns and pork, then season to taste with salt, pepper and sugar. Toss well and garnish with spring onion.

NUTRITION PER SERVE
*Protein 45 g; Fat 10 g; Carbohydrate 70 g; Dietary Fibre 6 g; Cholesterol 155 mg; 2415 kJ (575 cal)*

# Noodle Rösti

*Preparation time:*
*25 minutes*
*Total cooking time:*
*35 minutes*
*Makes 12*

*250 g (8 oz) dried*
*egg noodles*
*2 teaspoons sesame*
*oil*
*2 tablespoons toasted*
*sesame seeds*
*1 teaspoon salt*
*2 cloves garlic, crushed*
*2 teaspoons finely*
*grated fresh ginger*
*1 onion, finely chopped*
*2 tablespoons chopped*
*fresh chives*
*olive oil, for cooking*

1. Cook the noodles in salted boiling water for 6–8 minutes, or until tender. Drain and toss with all other ingredients except the olive oil.
2. Grease a large, non-stick frying pan with a tablespoon of olive oil; place over high heat. Take ¹/2 cup (30 g/1 oz) of the noodle mixture and use both hands to wind the noodles around, shaping them into small 'nests'.
3. Place several rösti in the hot pan and, using a spatula, gently press them down to a 2 cm (³/4 inch) thickness. Cook for 2–3 minutes on each side, or until the base is golden, drizzling a little oil around the edges so the noodles don't dry out.
4. Drain the rösti on paper towels and keep warm in the oven while cooking the remaining batches. Serve warm as a side dish, or make the rösti smaller and serve with good soy sauce as a starter.

NUTRITION PER RÖSTI
*Protein 3 g; Fat 4 g; Carbohydrate 15 g; Dietary Fibre 1 g; Cholesterol 4 mg; 460 kJ (110 cal)*

**Note:** To toast sesame seeds, simply toss them in a hot frying pan until they start to pop. You won't need any oil.

*Singapore Noodles (top) with Noodle Rösti*

# Chilli-Crusted Chicken Noodles

*Preparation time:*
25 minutes
*Total cooking time:*
20 minutes
*Serves 4–6*

1¹/2 teaspoons chilli
 powder
3 tablespoons cornflour
1¹/2 teaspoons salt
2 tablespoons oil
350 g (11¹/4 oz) chicken
 thigh fillets, sliced
4 spring onions, sliced
1 carrot, sliced
1 stick celery, sliced
2 tablespoons mirin or
 sherry
500 g (1 lb) Hokkien
 noodles, gently pulled
 apart
2 tablespoons oyster
 sauce
250 g (8 oz) baby bok
 choy, washed, trimmed,
 leaves separated

1. Combine the chilli
powder, cornflour and
salt; mix well. Heat the
oil in a wok over high
heat. Coat 5 chicken
strips in the mixture
and fry for 3 minutes,
or until golden. Drain
on paper towels and
repeat until finished.
Remove and set aside.
2. Reheat the wok over
medium heat. Add the
spring onions, carrot

and celery and stir-fry
for 1 minute. Add the
mirin and the noodles,
tossing well with a pair
of wooden spoons
until softened.
3. Add the oyster sauce
and 2 tablespoons water;
cover and steam for
2–4 minutes, or until
the noodles are tender.
4. Add the chicken and
bok choy and toss well.
Cover and steam for
30 seconds only. Serve
immediately.

NUTRITION PER SERVE
*Protein 15 g; Fat 9 g;
Carbohydrate 30 g; Dietary
Fibre 3 g; Cholesterol
40 mg; 1165 kJ (275 cal)*

# Tangy Capsicum Soba Noodles

*Preparation time:*
15 minutes
*Total cooking time:*
12 minutes
*Serves 4*

*Tangy Dressing*
3 tablespoons light soy
 sauce
1 tablespoon sesame oil
1 tablespoon white
 vinegar
1 teaspoon finely
 chopped fresh ginger
juice of 2 limes
3 tablespoons chopped
 fresh coriander
Tabasco sauce, to taste

2 red capsicums
1 small green capsicum
1 yellow capsicum
1 tablespoon sesame oil
250 g (8 oz) dried soba
 noodles
2 tablespoons toasted
 sesame seeds
3 tablespoons fresh
 coriander leaves

1. To make the tangy
dressing, mix together
the soy sauce, sesame
oil, vinegar, ginger, lime
juice, coriander and
Tabasco. Set aside.
2. Cut the capsicums
into strips about 5 mm
(¹/4 inch) thick. Heat
the sesame oil in a wok
or large pan, then fry
the capsicums over high
heat for 3–4 minutes,
or until partly cooked
but still bright. Set
aside and keep warm.
3. Cook the noodles in
plenty of boiling salted
water for 6 minutes, or
until tender. Drain well,
then add them to the
capsicum, pour on the
dressing and toss well.
Serve warm or at room
temperature, sprinkled
with sesame seeds and
coriander leaves.

NUTRITION PER SERVE
*Protein 10 g; Fat 15 g;
Carbohydrate 50 g; Dietary
Fibre 2 g; Cholesterol 0 mg;
1600 kJ (380 cal)*

**Note:** Light soy sauce is
saltier than regular soy,
and unlike the darker
soys, will not affect the
colour of a dish.

*Chilli-Crusted Chicken Noodles (top)
with Tangy Capsicum Soba Noodles*

# Crab and Noodle Mushrooms

*Preparation time:*
  20 minutes
*Total cooking time:*
  20 minutes
*Makes 6*

6 *flat mushrooms*
50 g (1³/4 oz) cellophane
  *noodles*
1 *tablespoon oil*
1 *clove garlic, crushed*
2 *teaspoons grated*
  *fresh ginger*
1 *small red chilli, finely*
  *chopped*
170 g (5¹/2 oz) can crab
  *meat, drained*
140 ml (4¹/2 fl oz) can
  *coconut cream*
¹/4 *cup (7 g/¹/4 oz) fresh*
  *coriander leaves*
2 *finely sliced red*
  *chillies, to garnish*
*lime wedges, to serve*

**1.** Preheat the oven
to moderate 180°C
(350°F/ Gas 4). Remove
the mushroom stems;
chop and set aside.
**2.** Soak the noodles in
hot water for 5 minutes,
or until soft. Drain and
cut into shorter lengths.
**3.** Heat the oil in a pan
over high heat. Add the
garlic, ginger and chilli;
cook for 30 seconds.
Add the crab meat and
mushroom stems and
cook for 1 minute. Toss
in the noodles, coconut
cream and coriander.
Season to taste.

**4.** Spoon the noodle
mixture evenly onto the
upturned mushrooms
and place in a greased
ovenproof dish, then
bake in the oven for
10–15 minutes. Garnish
with fine strips of red
chilli and serve with
lime wedges to squeeze
over the top.

NUTRITION PER SERVE
*Protein 5 g; Fat 8 g;
Carbohydrate 3 g; Dietary
Fibre 1 g; Cholesterol
25 mg; 435 kJ (105 cal)*

# Vermicelli, Beef and Thai Basil Salad

*Preparation time:*
  20 minutes +
  20 minutes soaking
*Total cooking time:*
  10–15 minutes
*Serves 4*

125 g (4 oz) dried
  *rice vermicelli*
600 g (1¹/4 lb) rump
  *steak*
2 *tablespoons oil*
2–3 *cloves garlic, thinly*
  *sliced*
1 *small red chilli, finely*
  *chopped (optional)*
1 *small red capsicum,*
  *thinly sliced*
1 *red onion, thinly*
  *sliced*
1 *cup (30 g/1 oz) fresh*
  *coriander leaves*
1 *cup (30 g/1 oz) fresh*
  *Thai basil leaves or*
  *green basil leaves*

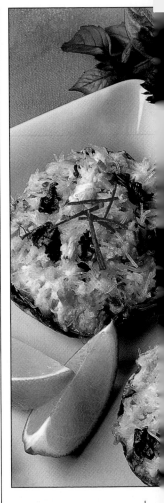

**Dressing**
1–2 *cloves garlic, crushed*
1 *red chilli, chopped*
2 *tablespoons soy sauce*
2 *tablespoons lime juice*
1 *tablespoon fish sauce*
3 *tablespoons grated*
  *palm sugar*

**1.** Soak the noodles in
hot water for 5 minutes,
or until soft. Drain.

*Crab and Noodle Mushrooms (left) with Vermicelli, Beef and Thai Basil Salad*

**2.** Combine the dressing ingredients; mix well and set aside.
**3.** Thinly slice the beef across the grain. Heat half the oil in a wok over high heat. Stir-fry the beef in 2–3 batches for 2 minutes, or until just brown, yet still pink in patches. (Ensure the wok is hot before each addition.) Remove the beef and set aside.
**4.** Heat the remaining oil in the wok, then stir-fry the garlic, chilli, capsicum and red onion for 2–3 minutes, or until soft but not browned.
**5.** Add the beef to just heat through quickly, then toss the mixture through the vermicelli. Pour on the dressing, and toss through the coriander and Thai basil leaves.

NUTRITION PER SERVE
*Protein 40 g; Fat 15 g; Carbohydrate 35 g; Dietary Fibre 2 g; Cholesterol 100 mg; 1795 kJ (425 cal)*

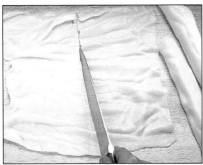

1  *Carefully unroll a rice noodle roll, then cut it in half using a sharp knife.*

2  *Place some prawns, then the other ingredients, neatly along the cut edge.*

# Steamed Seafood Rolls

*Preparation time:*
40 minutes
*Total cooking time:*
15–20 minutes
*Serves 4–6*

*Soy and Ginger Sauce*
3 tablespoons light soy
  sauce
2 cm (³/4 inch) piece
  fresh ginger, finely
  chopped
2 cloves garlic, finely
  crushed
1 teaspoon sugar

6 *Chinese broccoli
  leaves, finely shredded*
4 *fresh rice noodle rolls*
24 *raw prawns, peeled
  and deveined*
3 *cloves garlic, crushed*
3 cm (1¹/4 inch) piece
  fresh ginger, finely
  chopped
5 spring onions, finely
  sliced

**1.** To make the soy and ginger sauce, combine all the ingredients, mix well and set aside.
**2.** Steam the Chinese broccoli leaves until just wilted. Set aside.
**3.** Carefully unroll a rice noodle roll and cut it in half. Place 3 prawns and a little garlic and ginger on the cut-end of each half, but not all the way to the end. Top with some spring onion and Chinese broccoli. Fold both sides of the noodle in towards the centre, then roll up the noodle like a spring roll. Cover with a slightly damp tea towel while preparing the rest of the rolls.
**4.** Place 3–4 rolls in a large bamboo steamer lined with baking paper. Place over a wok or pan of boiling water and steam for 7–10 minutes, or until the prawns are cooked.

Remove the rolls, cover with foil and keep them warm while cooking the remainder. Serve warm with the soy and ginger sauce.

**Note:** Fresh rice noodle rolls are also known as plain rice noodle rolls. They are sold in packs of 4–6, and roll out into a long sheet. It is essential that the rolls you buy are very fresh. To check that they are, press them gently: they should feel soft and squishy. If not, they will be very hard to unroll, and may even crack. If you are using the rolls the same day or 1 day after purchase, there is no need to refrigerate them. If they have been refrigerated, leave them out overnight to soften before using.

NUTRITION PER ROLL
*Protein 20 g; Fat 1 g;
Carbohydrate 6 g; Dietary
Fibre 3 g; Cholesterol
115 mg; 450 kJ (105 cal)*

Steamed Seafood Rolls

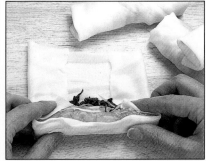

*3  Fold both sides in towards the centre,
then roll the noodle up like a spring roll.*

*4  Place 3–4 rolls in a bamboo steamer
lined with baking paper.*

## Curried Sunset Vegetable Noodles

*Preparation time:*
20 minutes
*Total cooking time:*
20 minutes
*Serves 4–6*

2 tablespoons oil
1¹/2 tablespoons
  Madras curry paste
1 small onion, sliced
500 g (1 lb) mix of
  pumpkin, carrot and
  parsnip, sliced into
  slender batons
¹/2 cup (125 ml/4 fl oz)
  coconut cream
¹/2 red capsicum, cut
  into long strips
2 teaspoons brown
  sugar
500 g (1 lb) Hokkien
  noodles, gently pulled
  apart
2 tablespoons lime juice
3 tablespoons lime
  pickle, finely chopped

1. Heat the oil in a
wok. Add the curry
paste and onion and
cook over low heat for
7 minutes, stirring often.
2. Add the pumpkin,
carrot and parsnip, and
2 tablespoons water.
Toss well, then cover
and cook for 5 minutes,
or until the vegetables
are just tender.
3. Add the coconut
cream, capsicum and
sugar, season to taste,
and simmer, uncovered,
for 2 minutes.

4. Add the noodles and
toss for 2–3 minutes, or
until the noodles are
softened and warmed
through. Transfer to
serving bowls, drizzle
with lime juice and top
with a little lime pickle.

NUTRITION PER SERVE
*Protein 6 g; Fat 15 g;
Carbohydrate 30 g; Dietary
Fibre 4 g; Cholesterol 0 mg;
1115 kJ (265 cal)*

## Soy Chicken and Crispy Noodles

*Preparation time:*
30 minutes
*Total cooking time:*
35 minutes
*Serves 4–6*

750 g (1¹/2 lb) chicken
  thigh fillets
3 teaspoons cornflour
¹/3 cup (80 ml/2³/4 fl oz)
  soy sauce
oil, for deep-frying
100 g (3¹/4 oz) dried
  rice vermicelli
1 clove garlic, crushed
2 teaspoons grated
  fresh ginger
1 carrot, sliced
2 sticks celery, sliced
1 red capsicum, sliced
1 green capsicum, sliced
100 g (3¹/4 oz) snow
  peas, trimmed
6 spring onions, sliced
¹/4 cup (60 ml/2 fl oz)
  chicken stock

1. Cut the chicken into
2 cm (³/4 inch) cubes.
Mix the cornflour into
half the soy sauce; add
the chicken, then cover
and refrigerate until
ready to use.
2. Heat the oil in a
large pan. Break the
vermicelli into small
pieces. Drop a noodle
into the oil: if it fizzes
and puffs, the oil is hot
enough. Add the noodles
in small amounts and
cook until puffed and
white. Drain on paper
towels and set aside.
3. Heat 1 tablespoon
of oil in a wok, add the
chicken and stir-fry in
batches over high heat
for about 4 minutes, or
until cooked. Remove
the chicken from the
wok and set aside.
4. Heat 1 tablespoon
of oil in the wok and
cook the garlic and
ginger for 30 seconds.
Add the vegetables and
cook, tossing well, for
2–3 minutes.
5. Add the chicken,
stock and remaining
soy sauce, and stir until
boiled and thickened.
Transfer to the centre
of serving plates and
arrange the noodles
around the edge.

NUTRITION PER SERVE
*Protein 30 g; Fat 9 g;
Carbohydrate 20 g; Dietary
Fibre 2 g; Cholesterol
85 mg; 1150 kJ (275 cal)*

*Curried Sunset Vegetable Noodles (top)
with Soy Chicken and Crispy Noodles*

## Asparagus and Sesame Noodles

*Preparation time:*
15 minutes
*Total cooking time:*
15 minutes
*Serves 4*

2 eggs, lightly beaten
400 g (12³/4 oz) fresh
  egg noodles
1 tablespoon rice wine
  vinegar
2 tablespoons kecap
  manis
2 teaspoons grated
  fresh ginger
1 teaspoon sesame oil
3 tablespoons olive oil
150 g (5 oz) asparagus,
  finely sliced
1 red capsicum, sliced
2 spring onions, sliced
2 tablespoons toasted
  sesame seeds

**1.** Lightly season the eggs and heat an oiled omelette pan. Cook an omelette over medium heat until the base is golden; turn and cook until just set. Cool and cut into long thin strips.
**2.** Cook the noodles in salted boiling water for 4 minutes; drain well.
**3.** Combine the vinegar, kecap manis, ginger and sesame oil. Set aside.
**4.** Heat the oil in a wok. Stir-fry the vegetables for 3 minutes over high heat. Add the noodles and sauce mixture and stir-fry until hot. Serve scattered with egg strips and sesame seeds.

NUTRITION PER SERVE
*Protein 10 g; Fat 20 g;
Carbohydrate 30 g; Dietary
Fibre 3 g; Cholesterol
90 mg; 1550 kJ (370 cal)*

## Udon with Ginger-Pork and Pickles

*Preparation time:*
30 minutes +
  20 minutes marinating
*Total cooking time:*
25 minutes
*Serves 4*

10 cm (4 inch) piece
  fresh ginger, peeled
pinch of sugar
200 g (6¹/2 oz) pork
  loin
500 g (1 lb) dried udon
  noodles
2 tablespoons cornflour
2 tablespoons oil
4 spring onions, sliced
150 g (5 oz) broccoli,
  cut in fine long florets
100 g (3¹/4 oz) Chinese
  pickled vegetables,
  finely sliced
3 tablespoons soy sauce
3 tablespoons mirin or
  sherry
1 Lebanese cucumber,
  halved and finely sliced
2 tablespoons toasted
  sesame seeds

**1.** Slice one third of the ginger paper-thin and place in a bowl; finely grate the rest. Squeeze the grated ginger over the ginger slices and discard the dry pulp. Season well with salt, pepper and sugar.
**2.** Cut the pork into 5 cm (2 inch) strips. Add to the ginger. Mix well; marinate for 20 minutes.
**3.** Cook the noodles in plenty of salted boiling water for 12 minutes, or until tender. Drain, rinse and set aside.
**4.** Remove the ginger from the pork. Scatter the cornflour over the pork and mix well. Heat half the oil in a wok over medium-high heat. Quickly stir-fry the pork until golden, adding the ginger at the end. Remove and set aside.
**5.** Heat the remaining oil; stir-fry the spring onion, broccoli and pickles for 30 seconds. Add 1 tablespoon of water, then cover and steam for 30 seconds.
**6.** Add the noodles, soy sauce and mirin, toss well and cook until heated. Add the pork and ginger and toss well. Divide between bowls, garnish with cucumber and sesame seeds and serve at once.

NUTRITION PER SERVE
*Protein 30 g; Fat 15 g;
Carbohydrate 105 g; Dietary
Fibre 4 g; Cholesterol
25 mg; 2880 kJ (685 cal)*

*Asparagus and Sesame Noodles (top)
with Udon with Ginger-Pork and Pickles*

# Vegetarian Lentil Combo

*Preparation time:*
15 minutes
*Total cooking time:*
40 minutes
*Serves 4*

1 tablespoon oil
1 large onion, finely
   chopped
2 cloves garlic, finely
   chopped
1 teaspoon ground
   cumin
1 teaspoon ground
   coriander
3/4 cup (185 g/6 oz)
   red lentils
2 large carrots, grated
440 g (14 oz) can
   tomatoes, chopped,
   liquid reserved
1 cup (250 ml/8 fl oz)
   vegetable stock
375 g (12 oz) fresh
   thick egg noodles
1 large zucchini, grated
3 tablespoons chopped
   fresh coriander
2 tablespoons lemon
   juice
fresh coriander leaves,
   to garnish

**1.** Heat the oil in a
heavy-based pan over
medium-low heat. Cook
the onion, garlic and
ground spices for about
8 minutes, stirring often.
Add the lentils, carrot,
tomato, tomato liquid
and stock; season well.
Stirring, bring to the
boil, then reduce the
heat, cover and simmer
for 25 minutes, or until
the lentils are tender.
**2.** Cook the noodles in
salted boiling water for
4 minutes or until tender.
Drain and keep warm.
**3.** Add the zucchini,
coriander and lemon
juice to the lentils.
Season to taste.
**4.** Divide the noodles
between bowls and
gently toss through
some lentil sauce. Top
with more sauce, garnish
with coriander leaves
and serve immediately.

NUTRITION PER SERVE
*Protein 20 g; Fat 7 g;
Carbohydrate 50 g; Dietary
Fibre 15 g; Cholesterol 0 mg;
1490 kJ (355 cal)*

# Soba Salad and Roasted Shallots

*Preparation time:*
20 minutes
*Total cooking time:*
1 hour
*Serves 4*

100 g (3 1/4 oz) Asian
   shallots, washed
1 teaspoon olive oil
200 g (6 1/2 oz) broccoli
   florets, lightly cooked
400 g (13 oz) tomatoes,
   seeded and diced
1 green chilli, finely
   sliced
250 g (8 oz) dried soba
   noodles
2 teaspoons black
   sesame seeds

*Dressing*
1/3 cup (80 ml/2 3/4 fl oz)
   rice wine vinegar
1/3 cup (80 ml/2 3/4 fl oz)
   light soy sauce
1 teaspoon sesame oil
1 tablespoon finely
   chopped fresh ginger
1 clove garlic, crushed

**1.** Preheat the oven to
moderate 180°C (350°F/
Gas 4). Put the unpeeled

*Vegetarian Lentil Combo (left) with Soba Salad and Roasted Shallots*

shallots in a non-metal, ovenproof dish. Toss with olive oil to coat. Roast for 1 hour or until the flesh inside is very soft. Cool, then squeeze out the segments and discard the skins.
**2.** Combine the dressing ingredients in a bowl. Add the broccoli, tomato and chilli and toss gently.

**3.** Cook the noodles in plenty of boiling salted water for 5 minutes, or until tender. Rinse, drain and divide among bowls. Spoon on the broccoli, tomato and chilli pieces, then drizzle the dressing all over. Arrange the roasted shallots on top and sprinkle with sesame seeds to serve.

NUTRITION PER SERVE: *Protein 10 g; Fat 5 g; Carbohydrate 50 g; Dietary Fibre 4 g; Cholesterol 0 mg; 1250 kJ (295 cal)*

**Note:** Black sesame seeds can be found in Japanese and some Asian food stores. If they are hard to find, use regular white sesame seeds instead.

23

# Spicy Seafood Laksa

*Preparation time:*
1 hour +
20 minutes soaking
*Total cooking time:*
1 hour 10 minutes
*Serves 4*

*4–5 large dried red
  chillies
500 g (1 lb) raw prawns
10 candlenuts
1 red onion, roughly
  chopped
5 cm (2 inch) piece
  galangal, peeled and
  roughly chopped
4 stems lemon grass,
  white part only, sliced
3 medium fresh red
  chillies, seeded and
  roughly chopped
2 teaspoons shrimp paste
2 teaspoons grated
  fresh turmeric or
  1 teaspoon powdered
3 tablespoons oil
2 cups (500 ml/16 fl oz)
  coconut milk
8 ready-made fried fish
  balls, sliced
400 g (13 oz) fresh
  rice spaghetti (laksa
  noodles)
2 small Lebanese
  cucumbers, cut into
  short, thin strips
100 g (3 1/4 oz) bean
  sprouts, scraggly ends
  removed
1/2 cup (10 g/1/4 oz)
  Vietnamese mint
  leaves or coriander*

*Spicy Seafood Laksa*

**1.** Soak the dried chillies in hot water for about 20 minutes.
**2.** Set aside 4 prawns. Peel the rest, reserving the prawns and placing the heads, shells, tails and legs in a deep heavy-based pan, without any oil. Cook over medium heat, shaking the pan now and then, for about 10 minutes, or until the shells are aromatic and a bright, dark orange.
**3.** Stir in 1 cup (250 ml/ 8 fl oz) water. When it has almost evaporated, stir in 1 more cup of water and bring to the boil, then add 1 litre water. (Adding the water very slowly in the initial stages will produce a rich, dark, flavoursome stock.)
**4.** Bring the stock to the boil, reduce the heat and simmer gently for 30 minutes. Add the 4 reserved prawns and cook until pink; remove and set aside. Strain the stock and discard the peelings. You should have between 2–3 cups (500–750 ml/16–24 fl oz) of stock.
**5.** Drain and chop the dried chillies and place in a food processor with the candlenuts, onion, galangal, lemon grass, fresh chillies, shrimp paste, turmeric and 2 tablespoons of the oil. Process into a paste, wiping down the sides of the bowl quite regularly with a spatula.
**6.** Heat the remaining oil in a wok and cook the paste over low heat for 8 minutes, or until very aromatic, stirring often. Stir in the prawn stock and coconut milk. Bring to the boil, then reduce the heat and simmer for 5 minutes. Add the shelled prawns and fish ball slices and simmer until the prawns turn pink.
**7.** Separate the noodles and cook them in boiling water for 30 seconds. (They will fall apart if overcooked.) Drain well and divide between deep soup bowls.
**8.** Ladle the soup over the noodles. Garnish with cucumber, bean sprouts, mint and a whole prawn. Serve at once, with the rest of the garnishes arranged on a plate for guests to help themselves.

NUTRITION PER SERVE
*Protein 35 g; Fat 45 g; Carbohydrate 30 g; Dietary Fibre 4 g; Cholesterol 190 mg; 2840 kJ (675 cal)*

**Notes:** Candlenuts should not be eaten raw. Fresh turmeric is an orange, ginger-like root, which should be peeled before grating. If laksa noodles are hard to find, any fresh thin rice noodle may be used.

## Pork and Rice-Noodle Cakes

*Preparation time:*
20 minutes
*Total cooking time:*
30 minutes
*Serves 6*

200 g (6¹/2 oz) dried
rice sticks
4 cloves garlic, finely
chopped
2 cm (³/4 inch) piece
fresh ginger, finely
chopped
200 g (6¹/2 oz) barbecued
pork, finely chopped
6 spring onions, finely
chopped
1 tablespoon soy sauce
1 teaspoon sugar
2 eggs, lightly beaten
oil, for cooking
sweet chilli sauce, for
serving

1. Soak the noodles
in hot water for about
5–10 minutes, or until
soft. Drain very well and
cut into short lengths.
2. Add the garlic, ginger,
pork and spring onion
and mix well. Combine
the soy sauce, sugar and
eggs; toss through the
noodles, coating well.
3. Heat enough oil to
cover the base of a large
frying pan. When the
oil is hot, cook ¹/4 cup
portions of the mixture
over medium-low heat
for about 5 minutes, or
until crisp and golden
underneath, then turn
and cook the other side
until golden. Drain on
paper towels and keep
warm while cooking
the remaining mixture.
Serve warm with some
sweet chilli sauce.

NUTRITION PER SERVE
*Protein 10 g; Fat 15 g;
Carbohydrate 35 g; Dietary
Fibre 2 g; Cholesterol
80 mg; 1320 kJ (315 cal)*

## Coriander, Coconut and Beef Burgers

*Preparation time:*
25 minutes
*Total cooking time:*
20 minutes
*Serves 4*

50 g (1³/4 oz) dried thin
udon or somen noodles
1 tablespoon fresh
coriander
1 cup (60 g/2 oz)
shredded coconut
350 g (11¹/4 oz) beef
mince
2 cloves garlic, crushed
¹/2 teaspoon finely
grated fresh ginger
2 teaspoons ground
coriander
1 teaspoon ground
cumin
¹/2 teaspoon paprika
2 eggs, lightly beaten
plain flour, for coating
¹/2 cup (125 ml/4 fl oz)
vegetable oil

*Sauce*
200 ml (6¹/2 fl oz)
bottled tomato pasta
sauce
1 large tomato, finely
chopped
1 teaspoon sambal
oelek, or to taste
1 tablespoon chopped
fresh Vietnamese mint

1. Cook the noodles
in salted boiling water
until tender. Drain,
rinse, drain again, and
mix in the coriander.
2. To make the sauce,
stir the ingredients in a
saucepan over medium
heat. Season to taste,
cover and keep warm.
3. Soak the coconut in
hot water for 3 minutes.
Drain. Add the beef,
garlic, ginger, spices and
eggs; season well. Mix
thoroughly, then divide
into 4 portions. Form a
cavity in each portion,
fill with noodles, fold
around and flatten
slightly into a burger.
Lightly roll in flour.
4. Heat the oil and
fry the burgers over
medium heat for about
5–6 minutes each side,
or until cooked through.
Drain on paper towels.
Serve with the sauce
and salad greens.

NUTRITION PER SERVE
*Protein 25 g; Fat 55 g;
Carbohydrate 35 g; Dietary
Fibre 6 g; Cholesterol
145 mg; 2995 kJ (715 cal)*

---

*Pork and Rice-Noodle Cakes (top)
with Coriander, Coconut and Beef Burgers*

1 Loosely separate the noodles and divide them into bundles.

2 Arrange the first bundle of noodles inside the larger basket.

## Prawn and Pea Noodle Baskets

*Preparation time:*
40 minutes
*Total cooking time:*
20–25 minutes
*Serves 4*

700 g (1 lb 7 oz) raw
    prawns
oil, for deep-frying
200 g (6¹/2 oz) fresh
    egg noodles
2 spring onions, chopped
1 clove garlic, crushed
¹/2 teaspoon finely
    grated fresh ginger
¹/2 teaspoon sesame oil
¹/2 teaspoon fish sauce
100 g (3¹/4 oz) green
    peas, cooked
3 tablespoons sliced
    water chestnuts
1 tablespoon fresh mint
2 teaspoons chopped
    fresh chives
80 g (2³/4 oz) snow pea
    sprouts
chive stalks, to garnish

1. Peel and devein the prawns; set aside.
2. Half-fill a deep-fryer or large pan with oil and heat to 180°C (350°F). Before the oil is too hot, dip in 2 wire baskets, one slightly smaller than the other; shake dry. Drop a noodle into the oil: if the oil bubbles and the noodle turns golden in 8–10 seconds, the oil is hot enough.
3. Separate the noodles; divide into 4 bundles. Arrange the first batch inside the large basket and press the smaller basket inside to mould the noodles. Holding the handles firmly, ease the baskets into the oil, keeping the noodles under. Gently twist the top basket to help stop sticking, tipping from side to side, and cook the noodles to an even golden brown. Drain on paper towels. Repeat with the other noodles.

4. Heat 2 tablespoons of oil in a wok. Stir-fry the prawns, spring onion, garlic and ginger over high heat for 2 minutes, or until the prawns turn pink. Stir in the sesame oil, fish sauce, peas and water chestnuts. Remove from the heat, season to taste and mix in the mint, chives and snow pea sprouts.
5. Pile the prawn and pea mixture into the noodle baskets, garnish with chive stalks and serve at once.

NUTRITION PER SERVE:
*Protein 40 g; Fat 15 g;
Carbohydrate 15 g; Dietary
Fibre 3 g; Cholesterol
260 mg; 1575 kJ (375 cal)*

**Note:** Wire baskets can be purchased from speciality kitchenware shops and come as a set that clip together. Before you arrange the noodles inside, make sure the baskets are well oiled to prevent the noodles sticking.

*Prawn and Pea Noodle Baskets*

*3 Fit the baskets together, hold firmly, then gently lower them into the oil.*

*4 Stir-fry the prawns over high heat until they just turn pink.*

# Chicken Noodle Soup

*Preparation time:*
15 minutes
*Total cooking time:*
20–25 minutes
*Serves 4*

1 tablespoon oil
4 chicken breast fillets
2 litres chicken stock
3 spring onions, sliced
100 g (3¹/4 oz) dried
 thin egg noodles,
 broken
³/4 cup (45 g/1¹/2 oz)
 chopped fresh parsley

**1.** Heat the oil in a large non-stick pan. Fry the chicken over medium-high heat for 15 minutes, or until golden, turning once. Remove from the pan, set aside to cool, then shred finely.
**2.** Bring the stock to the boil, then reduce the heat. Add the chicken, spring onion and noodles and simmer for 5–10 minutes, or until the noodles are tender. Season with salt and freshly ground pepper, stir through the parsley and serve immediately.

NUTRITION PER SERVE
*Protein 30 g; Fat 8 g; Carbohydrate 20 g; Dietary Fibre 1 g; Cholesterol 60 mg; 1155 kJ (275 cal)*

**Note:** For a much lighter soup, omit the shredded chicken.

# Chiang Mai Noodles

*Preparation time:*
25 minutes
*Total cooking time:*
15 minutes
*Serves 4*

**Nam Prik Sauce**
3 tablespoons fish sauce
1 tablespoon white
 vinegar
2–3 teaspoons finely
 chopped fresh red
 chillies
1 teaspoon sugar
2 teaspoons chopped
 fresh coriander stems

500 g (1 lb) fresh
 egg noodles
1 tablespoon oil
3 French or Asian
 shallots, finely sliced
6 cloves garlic, chopped
finely chopped red
 chilli, to taste
1–2 tablespoons red
 curry paste
350 g (11¹/4 oz) lean
 chicken or pork,
 finely sliced
1 carrot, finely sliced
2 tablespoons fish sauce
2 teaspoons brown sugar
3 spring onions, sliced
¹/4 cup (7 g/¹/4 oz) fresh
 coriander leaves

**1.** Combine all the nam prik sauce ingredients, stirring to dissolve the sugar. Set aside.

**2.** Cook the noodles in plenty of salted boiling water for 4 minutes, or until just tender. Drain well and keep the noodles warm.
**3.** Heat the oil in a wok or large frying pan. When the oil is very hot, add the shallots, garlic, chopped chilli and curry paste, and stir-fry for 2 minutes over high heat.
**4.** Add the meat in batches and cook each batch for 3 minutes, or until the meat just changes colour.
**5.** Return all the meat to the wok. Add the carrot, fish sauce and sugar. Stir well and bring to the boil.
**6.** Divide the noodles between serving bowls, then toss in the meat mixture and sliced spring onions. Garnish with coriander and serve at once with the nam prik sauce.

NUTRITION PER SERVE
*Protein 25 g; Fat 10 g; Carbohydrate 40 g; Dietary Fibre 4 g; Cholesterol 60 mg; 1490 kJ (355 cal)*

**Notes:** This dish must be served as soon as it is cooked or it will become soggy. Some brands of curry paste are hotter than others, so adjust the quantity to taste.

*Chicken Noodle Soup (top) with Chiang Mai Noodles*

# Tangy Prawn and Noodle Salad

*Preparation time:*
  20 minutes
*Total cooking time:*
  10 minutes
*Serves 4*

### Dressing
*2 cloves garlic, crushed*
*1 small red chilli, chopped*
*1 tablespoon oil*
*2 tablespoons fish sauce*
*3 tablespoons lime juice*
*1 teaspoon shrimp paste*
*20 g ($^3$/4 oz) grated palm sugar or brown sugar*

*100 g (3$^1$/4 oz) cellophane noodles*
*4 spring onions, sliced*
*375 g (12 oz) cooked prawns, peeled and deveined*
*$^1$/3 cup (10 g/$^1$/4 oz) chopped fresh coriander leaves*
*2 tablespoons salted beer nuts, chopped*

1. Combine all the dressing ingredients, stirring well to dissolve the sugar. Set aside.
2. Cook the noodles in plenty of boiling water for 10 minutes, or until tender. Rinse, drain, and cut into shorter lengths.
3. Add the dressing to the noodles and mix well. Toss through the spring onions, prawns and coriander. Transfer to serving bowls and sprinkle with nuts. Serve at room temperature.

NUTRITION PER SERVE
*Protein 30 g; Fat 10 g; Carbohydrate 10 g; Dietary Fibre 4 g; Cholesterol 180 mg; 1080 kJ (255 cal)*

# Garlic Chive, Egg and Crispy Pork Noodles

*Preparation time:*
  25 minutes
*Total cooking time:*
  15 minutes
*Serves 4*

*2 eggs, beaten*
*1 tablespoon oil*
*150 g (5 oz) barbecue pork, finely cubed*
*1 small red onion, cut into fine slithers*
*2 cloves garlic, finely chopped*
*500 g (1 lb) fresh thick rice noodles*
*1 tablespoon soy sauce*
*2 teaspoons sesame oil*
*2 teaspoons hoisin sauce*
*30 g (1 oz) chopped garlic chives*

1. Heat a small, lightly greased non-stick frying pan. Pour in the egg, swirl the pan until set, then cook on medium heat for 1 minute, or until the base is golden. Turn over and cook for 30 seconds. Remove, cool slightly, then cut into thin strips.
2. Heat the oil in a wok and stir-fry the pork over medium heat for about 3 minutes, or until golden and crisp. Remove and set aside.
3. Add the onion and garlic to the wok and cook for 3 minutes, or until soft.
4. Add the noodles, soy sauce, sesame oil and hoisin sauce and gently toss to coat. Cover and steam for 2 minutes, or until the mixture is heated through, ensuring the noodles don't burn.
5. Add the pork and half the garlic chives; toss well. Transfer to serving plates, sprinkle with the egg strips and remaining garlic chives, and serve immediately.

NUTRITION PER SERVE
*Protein 15 g; Fat 15 g; Carbohydrate 30 g; Dietary Fibre 3 g; Cholesterol 115 mg; 1350 kJ (320 cal)*

**Note:** Fresh rice noodles should be left to soften at room temperature for at least 30 minutes before use, or they will break during cooking. Barbecue pork, also known as char sui, is widely sold in speciality shops in Chinatown regions, and freezes for up to 3 months.

*Tangy Prawn and Noodle Salad (top) with Garlic Chive, Egg and Crispy Pork Noodles*

# Sweet and Sour Potato Noodles

*Preparation time:*
30 minutes
*Total cooking time:*
15 minutes
*Serves 4*

1 tablespoon oil
5 cm (2 inch) piece fresh
 ginger, sliced paper-thin
1 large onion, cut into
 fine wedges
1 large carrot, sliced
1 red capsicum, sliced
1 cup (160 g/5$^1$/4 oz)
 diced fresh pineapple
1 tablespoon brown
 sugar
1 tablespoon balsamic
 vinegar
$^1$/3 cup (80 ml/2$^3$/4 fl oz)
 Chinese cooking wine
340 g (11 oz) thin
 potato noodles
$^1$/2 Lebanese cucumber,
 thinly sliced
30 g (1 oz) pickled
 ginger

1. Heat the oil in a wok.
Add the ginger, onion,
carrot and capsicum
and stir-fry over low
heat for 2–3 minutes.
2. Add the pineapple,
sugar and vinegar; cook
for 4 minutes, stirring
occasionally. Add the
cooking wine, stirring
well. Leave to simmer.
3. Cook the noodles in
plenty of boiling salted
water for 5 minutes, or
until translucent and
tender. Drain, transfer

to bowls and arrange
the vegetables on top.
Serve with the cucumber
and pickled ginger.

NUTRITION PER SERVE
*Protein 5 g; Fat 5 g;
Carbohydrate 45 g; Dietary
Fibre 6 g; Cholesterol 0 mg;
1060 kJ (250 cal)*

**Note:** Pickled ginger is
sold in Asian food stores
and has a lovely taste.

# Chicken and Prawn Tonkatsu

*Preparation time:*
 25 minutes
*Total cooking time:*
 15 minutes
*Serves 4*

250 g (8 oz) fresh
 egg noodles
2 tablespoons oil
2 chicken breast fillets,
 thinly sliced
100 g (3$^1$/4 oz) bacon
 or barbecue pork,
 diced
12 raw prawns, peeled
 and deveined, tails
 intact
6 spring onions, sliced
1 celery stick, sliced
1 carrot, sliced
2 cups (90 g/3 oz) sliced
 Chinese cabbage
100 g (3$^1$/4 oz) green
 beans or snow peas,
 sliced
90 g (3 oz) bean sprouts

*Tonkatsu Dressing*
3 tablespoons Tonkatsu
 or barbecue sauce
1 tablespoon light soy
 sauce
1 tablespoon mirin or
 sake
1 tablespoon grated
 fresh ginger
1 tablespoon sugar

1. Cook the noodles in
plenty of boiling salted
water for 4–5 minutes,
or until tender, stirring
often. Drain, rinse, drain
again and set aside.
2. Combine all the
dressing ingredients,
mix well and set aside.
3. Heat the oil in a wok
over high heat. Stir-fry
the chicken and bacon
or pork for 2–3 minutes,
or until the chicken is
nearly cooked. Add the
prawns and cook until
they just change colour.
4. Add the vegetables,
reserving some of the
spring onion for the
garnish. Heat, stirring,
for 2–3 minutes, or
until the vegetables
are slightly soft.
5. Toss through the
dressing and noodles;
stir for 1 minute to heat
through. Garnish with
the reserved spring onion
and serve at once.

NUTRITION PER SERVE
*Protein 35 g; Fat 15 g;
Carbohydrate 30 g; Dietary
Fibre 5 g; Cholesterol
130 mg; 1725 kJ (410 cal)*

*Sweet and Sour Potato Noodles (top)
with Chicken and Prawn Tonkatsu*

1 *Slit the shelled prawns open along the back, then carefully pull out the vein.*

2 *Using a sharp knife, cut the noodles the same length as the prawn body.*

# Japanese Prawn, Noodle and Seaweed Parcels

*Preparation time:*
  45 minutes
*Total cooking time:*
  10 minutes
*Makes 24*

24 raw prawns
250 g (8 oz) dried
  somen noodles
4 sheets dried seaweed
*1/2 cup (60 g/2 oz) plain
  flour*
2 egg yolks
oil, for deep-frying

**Dipping Sauce**
*1/3 cup (80 ml/2 3/4 fl oz)
  Tonkatsu sauce or
  barbecue sauce
2 tablespoons lemon
  juice
1 tablespoon sake or
  mirin
1–2 teaspoons grated
  fresh ginger*

1. Shell the prawns, leaving the tail intact. Slit the prawns halfway through along the back and remove the vein. Set aside.
2. Using a sharp knife, cut the noodles to the same length as the prawn bodies, to the base of the tail. Keep the noodles in neat bundles and set aside. Cut the seaweed into 2.5 cm (1 inch) strips.
3. Sift the flour into a bowl. Mix the egg yolks with 3 tablespoons water, then whisk the mixture into the flour and beat to a smooth batter. Add another tablespoon of water if the mixture is too thick. Set aside.
4. Combine the dipping sauce ingredients, adding the ginger to taste. Mix well and set aside.
5. Half-fill a deep-fryer or large pan with oil and heat to 180° (350°F).

6. Dip a prawn in the batter, letting the excess run off. Roll the prawn lengthways in noodles to coat it with a single layer; secure the noodles by rolling a seaweed strip around the centre of the prawn, securing the seaweed with a little batter. Repeat with the rest of the prawns.
7. Drop a cube of bread into the oil: if it browns in 5 seconds, the oil is hot enough. Deep-fry 2–3 coated prawns at a time for about 1 minute. Drain on paper towels and keep warm while cooking the remainder. Serve warm with the dipping sauce.

NUTRITION PER SERVE
*Protein 6 g; Fat 2 g;
Carbohydrate 10 g; Dietary
Fibre 0 g; Cholesterol
45 mg; 375 kJ (90 cal)*

**Note:** Seaweed sheets (nori) and Tonkatsu sauce are sold by Japanese and some Asian food suppliers.

---

*Japanese Prawn, Noodle and Seaweed Parcels*

*3  Neatly roll the batter-dipped prawn in noodles, and wrap with a seaweed strip.*

*4  Deep-fry the prawn and noodle parcels until golden.*

# Peanut and Sesame Noodles

*Preparation time:*
15 minutes
*Total cooking time:*
15 minutes
*Serves 4*

3 tablespoons toasted
sesame seeds
2/3 cup (160 g/5¹/4 oz)
crunchy peanut butter
2 tablespoons sweet
chilli sauce, and extra
for serving
3 teaspoons soy sauce
3 teaspoons sesame oil
2 teaspoons rice wine
vinegar
1 tablespoon lemon
juice
750 g (1¹/2 lb) Hokkien
noodles, separated
6 spring onions, cut
into very fine strips

**1.** Using a mortar and
pestle, grind the sesame
seeds to a powder. Place
in a frying pan over
very low heat.
**2.** Add the peanut butter,
the liquid ingredients,
3 tablespoons water
and a pinch of freshly
ground black pepper.
Stir for 2–3 minutes, or
until the sauce blends
together and warms
through, taking care
it doesn't burn. If the
sauce becomes too
thick, stir in 3 more
tablespoons water.
Set aside, cover and
keep warm.

**3.** Heat 4 tablespoons
water in a wok, add the
noodles and toss well.
Cover and steam for
3–4 minutes, or until
soft and plump. Transfer
to serving bowls, drizzle
with the warm sauce,
then top with spring
onion and extra sweet
chilli sauce if desired.

NUTRITION PER SERVE
*Protein 20 g; Fat 30 g;
Carbohydrate 60 g; Dietary
Fibre 9 g; Cholesterol 0 mg;
2465 kJ (585 cal)*

**Note:** To add a truly
authentic flavour to this
wonderful dish, use
freshly made peanut
butter, which you can
grind yourself in many
health-food shops.

# Easy Spinach, Mushroom and Chicken Stir-fry

*Preparation time:*
15 minutes
*Total cooking time:*
20 minutes
*Serves 4*

**Dressing**
1 teaspoon chopped
fresh ginger
2 teaspoons sugar
1 tablespoon rice wine
vinegar
2 tablespoons hoisin
sauce

250 g (8 oz) dried udon
noodles
2 tablespoons peanut oil
300 g (10 oz) chicken
breast fillet, thinly
sliced
1 red capsicum, sliced
300 g (10 oz) Swiss
brown or button
mushrooms, halved
150 g (5 oz) oyster
mushrooms, halved
2 spring onions, finely
chopped
500 g (1 lb) English
spinach, washed and
roughly chopped

**1.** Mix together the
dressing ingredients.
Stir well and set aside.
**2.** Cook the noodles in
plenty of boiling salted
water for 10 minutes,
or until tender. Drain,
cover and keep warm.
**3.** Heat the oil in a wok
until sizzling. Stir-fry
the chicken over high
heat until just cooked.
Remove and set aside.
**4.** Add the capsicum,
mushrooms and spring
onions, and stir-fry for
3–4 minutes.
**5.** Add the dressing,
noodles, chicken and
spinach and stir-fry
until heated through,
and the spinach has just
wilted. Serve at once.

NUTRITION PER SERVE
*Protein 30 g; Fat 15 g;
Carbohydrate 55 g; Dietary
Fibre 8 g; Cholesterol
40 mg; 1985 kJ (470 cal)*

*Peanut and Sesame Noodles (top)
with Easy Spinach, Mushroom and Chicken Stir-fry*

## Phad Thai

*Preparation time:*
  30 minutes
*Total cooking time:*
  10–15 minutes
*Serves 4*

250 g (8 oz) dried thick
  rice stick noodles
2 tablespoons oil
3 cloves garlic, chopped
1–2 red chillies, chopped
150 g (5 oz) pork, finely
  sliced
100 g (3¹/4 oz) peeled
  raw prawns, deveined
  and chopped
75 g (2¹/2 oz) garlic
  chives, chopped
2 tablespoons fish sauce
2 tablespoons lime juice
2 teaspoons brown sugar
2 eggs, beaten
90 g (3 oz) bean sprouts
sprigs of fresh coriander,
  to garnish
3 tablespoons roasted
  peanuts, chopped

**1.** Soak the noodles in
hot water until soft.
Drain and set aside.
**2.** Heat the oil in a wok
over high heat. When
very hot, add the garlic,
chillies and pork, stirring
constantly for 2 minutes.
Add the prawns and
stir-fry for 3 minutes.
**3.** Add the chives and
noodles; cover and cook
for 1 minute. Add the
fish sauce, lime juice,
sugar and eggs and toss
well until hot. Serve
sprinkled with sprouts,
coriander and peanuts.

NUTRITION PER SERVE
*Protein 25 g; Fat 20 g;
Carbohydrate 55 g; Dietary
Fibre 2 g; Cholesterol
145 mg; 2035 kJ (485 cal)*

## Noodle Wedges
## with Pastrami

*Preparation time:*
  15 minutes
*Total cooking time:*
  20–25 minutes
*Serves 4*

250 g (8 oz) fresh
  egg noodles
oil, for cooking
1 leek, finely sliced
1 yellow capsicum, sliced
1 teaspoon finely
  chopped fresh ginger
1 garlic clove, crushed
¹/2 teaspoon dried chilli
  flakes
1 teaspoon sesame oil
2 tablespoons soy sauce
¹/2 cup (125 ml/4 fl oz)
  chicken stock
200 g (6¹/2 oz) firm or
  marinated tofu, diced
50 g (1³/4 oz) water
  chestnuts, thinly sliced
200 g (6¹/2 oz) pastrami,
  finely sliced
50 g (1³/4 oz) snow pea
  sprouts
3 tablespoons chopped
  toasted pecans

**1.** Cook the noodles in
plenty of salted boiling
water for 5 minutes,
or until tender. Rinse,
drain, stir in some oil,
then spread on a large
plate to cool.
**2.** Heat some oil in
a large non-stick pan,
swirling to coat the pan
well. Add the noodles
and cook over medium
heat for 5–7 minutes,
or until golden brown.
Turn onto a plate, oil
the pan and brown the
other side of the noodle
cake. Keep warm.
**3.** Heat 2 tablespoons
of oil in a wok. Stir-fry
the leek and capsicum
over medium heat for
3–4 minutes. Stir in the
ginger, garlic and chilli
flakes, add the sesame
oil and soy sauce and
cook for 10–12 seconds.
**4.** Increase the heat to
high. Add the stock,
tofu, chestnuts and
pastrami: stir until hot.
Remove from the heat,
toss in the snow pea
sprouts, transfer to a
warm plate and sprinkle
with pecans. Cut the
noodle cake into wedges
and serve with the
pastrami mixture.

NUTRITION PER SERVE
*Protein 15 g; Fat 55 g;
Carbohydrate 20 g; Dietary
Fibre 3 g; Cholesterol
225 mg; 2735 kJ (650 cal)*

**Note:** Marinated tofu
is sold in Asian grocery
stores and also in some
supermarkets.

*Phad Thai (top) and
Noodle Wedges with Pastrami*

# Duck and Mandarin Soup

*Preparation time:*
15 minutes
*Total cooking time:*
25 minutes
*Serves 4–5*

1 kg (2 lb) Chinese-
style roasted duck
2 litres chicken stock
1 onion, chopped
3 x 6 cm (2¹/2 inch)
strips orange rind
1 star anise
2 tablespoons chopped
fresh ginger
100 g (3¹/4 oz) instant
noodles, broken
310 g (10 oz) can
mandarin segments,
drained
3 tablespoons chopped
fresh coriander
2 spring onions, finely
sliced

1. Remove the meat from the duck. Discard the excess fat and chop the meat into 1 cm (¹/2 inch) pieces; cover and set aside. Roughly chop the skin and bones and place in a large pan with the stock, onion, orange rind, star anise and ginger. Bring to the boil, then reduce the heat, cover and simmer for about 15 minutes. Strain the stock into a clean pan.
2. Bring the stock to the boil. Add the noodles and boil for about 2 minutes. Add the duck meat and mandarin; reduce the heat and simmer for 2 minutes. Add the coriander and spring onion. Serve at once.

NUTRITION PER SERVE
Protein 45 g; Fat 55 g;
Carbohydrate 25 g; Dietary
Fibre 1 g; Cholesterol
245 mg; 3215 kJ (765 cal)

# Rice Noodles with Seafood, Chilli and Basil

*Preparation time:*
20 minutes +
30 minutes marinating
*Total cooking time:*
15 minutes
*Serves 4*

250 g (8 oz) raw prawns
150 g (5 oz) calamari
rings
250 g (8 oz) boneless,
firm fish
¹/2 cup (125 ml/4 fl oz)
olive oil
3 small red chillies,
seeded and finely sliced
3 cloves garlic, finely
chopped
2 tablespoons oil
2 tablespoons dry white
wine
500 g (1 lb) fresh thick
rice noodles
2 ripe tomatoes, diced
¹/2 cup (30 g/1 oz) fresh
chopped basil

1. Peel and devein the prawns. Cut any large calamari rings in half; cut the fish into bite-sized pieces. Combine the olive oil, chilli and garlic and add to the seafood. Cover and chill for 30 minutes.
2. Place the oil in a wok over high heat. When the oil is very hot, quickly stir-fry the seafood in 3–4 batches for about 2 minutes each. After removing each batch, ensure the wok is very hot before adding the next batch.
3. Add the wine and 4 tablespoons water to the wok; reduce the heat to low and add the noodles, tossing well to coat. Cover and steam for 2 minutes, or until the noodles are soft and plump—do not overcook them.
4. Add the seafood and any juices, season well and toss well. Add the tomatoes and basil; toss and serve immediately.

NUTRITION PER SERVE
Protein 35 g; Fat 40 g;
Carbohydrate 30 g; Dietary
Fibre 2 g; Cholesterol
210 mg; 2700 kJ (640 cal)

**Note:** Fresh rice noodles should be left to soften at room temperature for at least 30 minutes before use, or they will break during cooking.

---

*Duck and Mandarin Soup (top)
and Rice Noodles with Seafood, Chilli and Basil*

## Bok Choy and Chestnut Stir-fry

*Preparation time:*
*15 minutes*
*Total cooking time:*
*7 minutes*
*Serves 4*

*450 g (14 oz) Hokkien*
*noodles*
*1/2 cup (125 ml/4 fl oz)*
*chicken stock*
*2 tablespoons oyster*
*sauce*
*2 tablespoons light soy*
*sauce*
*1 tablespoon sesame oil*
*2 tablespoons olive oil*
*1 carrot, finely sliced*
*2 celery sticks, sliced*
*4 spring onions, sliced*
*3 baby bok choy,*
*washed and trimmed,*
*leaves separated*
*2 tablespoons finely*
*chopped fresh ginger*
*100 g (3 1/4 oz) snow*
*peas, sliced*
*90 g (3 oz) bean sprouts*
*1/2 cup (90 g/3 oz) water*
*chestnuts, chopped*

1. Soak the noodles in hot water for 1 minute. Drain well; set aside.
2. Combine the stock, oyster sauce, soy sauce and sesame oil; mix well.
3. Heat the olive oil in a wok over high heat. Add the carrot, celery, spring onion, bok choy and ginger; stir-fry for 2 minutes. Add the rest of the ingredients and stir-fry for 3–4 minutes. Serve at once.

NUTRITION PER SERVE
*Protein 8 g; Fat 15 g;*
*Carbohydrate 40 g; Dietary*
*Fibre 6 g; Cholesterol 0 mg;*
*1395 kJ (330 cal)*

## Teriyaki-style Chicken Noodles

*Preparation time:*
*25 minutes +*
*2 hours marinating*
*Total cooking time:*
*25 minutes*
*Serves 4–6*

*Teriyaki Marinade*
*3 tablespoons mirin*
*1/3 cup (80 ml/2 3/4 fl oz)*
*tamari or soy sauce*
*2 teaspoons sugar*
*3 cloves garlic, finely*
*chopped*
*3 cm (1 1/4 inch) piece*
*fresh ginger, finely*
*chopped*

*500 g (1 lb) chicken*
*thigh fillets, trimmed*
*500 g (1 lb) fresh or*
*dried Udon noodles*
*oil, for cooking*
*3 carrots, finely sliced*
*10 spring onions, sliced*
*3 tablespoons toasted*
*sesame seeds*
*dried chilli flakes and*
*extra sliced spring*
*onions, to garnish*

1. Combine the teriyaki marinade ingredients and mix well. Cut the chicken into strips and add to the marinade. Mix well, then cover and refrigerate for at least 2 hours.
2. Cook the noodles in plenty of boiling salted water for 10 minutes, or until just tender. Drain and rinse well.
3. Drain the chicken, reserving the marinade. Heat some oil in a wok over high heat. When the oil is hot, stir-fry the chicken in 2–3 batches for 3–4 minutes each, or until just cooked. Remove and set aside.
4. Heat some more oil in the wok and stir-fry the carrot and spring onion over high heat for 3–4 minutes. Add the drained noodles, tossing well until heated through, then remove and set aside.
5. Add the marinade to the wok and bring to the boil. Reduce the heat and simmer for 1–2 minutes to a thick glaze. Add the chicken, noodles, vegetables and sesame seeds, tossing to coat. Transfer to deep bowls, sprinkle with chilli flakes and extra sliced spring onion, and serve at once.

NUTRITION PER SERVE
*Protein 30 g; Fat 20 g;*
*Carbohydrate 75 g; Dietary*
*Fibre 4 g; Cholesterol*
*60 mg; 2440 kJ (580 cal)*

---

*Bok Choy and Chestnut Stir-fry (top)*
*with Teriyaki-style Chicken Noodles*

# Fried Crispy Noodles (Mee Grob)

*Preparation time:*
  30 minutes
*Total cooking time:*
  20 minutes
*Serves 4*

100 g (3¼ oz) dried
  rice vermicelli
2 cups (500 ml/16 fl oz)
  oil, for deep-frying
100 g (3¼ oz) tofu,
  cut into long fine
  strips
2 cloves garlic, finely
  chopped
4 cm (1½ inch) piece
  fresh ginger, grated
150 g (5 oz) chicken or
  pork mince
100 g (3¼ oz) peeled
  raw prawns, deveined
  and finely chopped
2 tablespoons fish sauce
1 tablespoon white
  vinegar
2 tablespoons soft
  brown sugar
2 tablespoons chilli
  sauce
1 teaspoon chopped
  red chillies
2 small heads pickled
  garlic, chopped
40 g (1¼ oz) garlic
  chives, chopped
1 cup (30 g/1 oz) fresh
  coriander leaves

**1.** Soak the vermicelli in a bowl of hot water for 1 minute; drain and leave to dry completely.
**2.** Heat the oil in a deep pan. Drop a bread cube into the oil: if it browns in 5 seconds, the oil is hot enough.
**3.** Add the tofu to the oil in several batches and cook over high heat for 1–2 minutes, or until golden and crisp. Remove and drain.
**4.** Add the noodles to the oil in small batches and cook for 10 seconds, or until crisp and puffy. Remove immediately to prevent the noodles absorbing too much oil. Drain on paper towels and allow to cool.
**5.** Heat 1 tablespoon oil in a wok over high heat. When hot, add the garlic, ginger, mince and prawns and stir-fry for about 2 minutes, or until the mixture is golden.
**6.** Add the fish sauce, vinegar, sugar, chilli sauce and chillies; stir until the mixture boils. Add the noodles and tofu, tossing well, then quickly toss through the pickled garlic, garlic chives and coriander. Serve at once, or the dish will become soggy.

NUTRITION PER SERVE
*Protein 15 g; Fat 20 g; Carbohydrate 30 g; Dietary Fibre 3 g; Cholesterol 60 mg; 1590 kJ (380 cal)*

**Note:** Whole heads of pickled garlic are sold in jars in many Asian food stores.

*Fried Crispy Noodles (Mee Grob)*

*1 Chop the red chillies and the heads of pickled garlic.*

*2 Deep-fry the tofu strips until golden and crisp.*

3  Deep-fry the dried rice vermicelli in
small batches until crisp and puffy.

4  Stir-fry the garlic, ginger, mince and
prawns over high heat until golden.

## Fragrant Chicken and Noodles

*Preparation time:*
 15 minutes
*Total cooking time:*
 20 minutes
*Serves 4*

2 tablespoons sugar
1/3 cup (80 ml/2³/4 fl oz)
 fish sauce
3 tablespoons oil
2 onions, chopped
2 teaspoons red curry
 paste
1 clove garlic, crushed
600 g (1¹/4 lb) chicken
 breast fillets, cut into
 strips
300 g (10 oz) instant
 noodles
4 spring onions, chopped
1¹/2 cups (45 g/1¹/2 oz)
 fresh coriander,
 chopped

1. Dissolve the sugar in the fish sauce. Mix well and set aside.
2. Place half the oil in a wok over high heat. When hot, stir-fry the onions for 3 minutes, or until soft. Remove the onions; set aside.
3. Over low heat, add the remaining oil and stir-fry the curry paste and garlic for 1 minute. Increase the heat to high, add the chicken and stir-fry for 10 minutes, or until lightly cooked.

4. Return the onions to the wok, reduce the heat and keep warm.
5. Cook the noodles in boiling water for about 2 minutes, or until tender. Drain and toss in the wok with the fish sauce, spring onion and coriander until heated through. Serve at once.

NUTRITION PER SERVE
*Protein 45 g; Fat 35 g;
Carbohydrate 60 g; Dietary
Fibre 2 g; Cholesterol
75 mg; 2950 kJ (700 cal)*

## Vietnamese Spring Rolls

*Preparation time:*
 50 minutes +
 15 minutes soaking
*Total cooking time:*
 Nil
*Makes 20*

20 large cooked prawns
50 g (1³/4 oz) cellophane
 noodles
20 rice paper wrappers
40 mint leaves
10 garlic chives, chopped
 in half

**Dipping Sauce**
1 tablespoon satay sauce
2 tablespoons hoisin
 sauce
1 fresh red chilli, finely
 chopped
1 tablespoon chopped
 roasted peanuts

1. Peel and devein the prawns, then cut the prawns in half along their length.
2. Mix together the ingredients for the dipping sauce. Stir well and set aside.
3. Soak the noodles for about 15 minutes in enough hot water to cover. Drain thoroughly and chop the noodles into shorter lengths.
4. Brush both sides of each wrapper with water using a pastry brush. Leave for about 2 minutes, or until soft and pliable. Stack the wrappers on top of each other, sprinkling each layer lightly with water to prevent the wrappers sticking together and drying out. (Handle the rice wrappers very gently, as they can tear easily when softened.)
5. Spoon 1 tablespoon of the chopped noodles along the bottom third of a softened wrapper, then top with 2 mint leaves, 2 prawn halves and half a garlic chive. Roll up the wrapper, leaving some of the garlic chive poking out the ends. Repeat with the remaining ingredients and serve with the dipping sauce.

NUTRITION PER SERVE
*Protein 4 g; Fat 1 g;
Carbohydrate 3 g; Dietary
Fibre 1 g; Cholesterol
30 mg; 150 kJ (35 cal)*

---

*Fragrant Chicken and Noodles (top)
with Vietnamese Spring Rolls*

## Warm Green Salad on Noodle Baskets

*Preparation time:*
30 minutes
*Total cooking time:*
20–25 minutes
*Serves 4*

2 tablespoons light
  soy sauce
2 tablespoons oyster
  sauce
1 tablespoon honey
150 g (5 oz) fresh thin
  egg noodles
oil, for deep-frying
2 cloves garlic, finely
  crushed
1 small red chilli, finely
  chopped
4 cm (1 1/2 inch) piece
  fresh ginger, peeled
  and grated
4 spring onions, sliced
100 g (3 1/4 oz)
  asparagus, sliced
1 small green capsicum,
  cut into chunks
1 cup (125 g/4 oz)
  sliced green beans
180 g (5 3/4 oz) baby
  corn, halved
1 cup (90 g/3 oz) bean
  sprouts
1 cup (45 g/1 1/2 oz)
  thinly sliced Chinese
  cabbage
1 tablespoon sesame
  seeds, lightly toasted

**1.** Combine the soy
sauce, oyster sauce and
honey and set aside.

**2.** Half-fill a deep-fryer
or large pan with oil and
heat to 180°C (350°F).
Before the oil is hot, dip
in 2 wire strainers (one
slightly smaller than the
other) and shake dry.
Drop a noodle into the
oil: if the oil bubbles
and the noodle turns
golden in 8–10 seconds,
the oil is hot enough.
**3.** Divide the noodles
into 4 bundles. Arrange
a batch inside the large
strainer; press the small
strainer inside. Holding
the handles firmly, lower
the noodles into the oil.
Gently twist the top
strainer to stop sticking,
tipping from side to
side. Cook until golden.
Drain and repeat with
the remaining noodles.
**4.** Heat 2 tablespoons
oil in a wok. Stir-fry the
garlic, chilli, ginger and
spring onion on medium
heat for 1 minute.
**5.** Increase the heat to
high. Add the aparagus,
capsicum, beans and
corn and stir-fry for
2–3 minutes. Add the
sprouts and cabbage,
cook for 1 minute, add
the soy sauce mixture
and toss well. Dish into
the baskets, sprinkle
with sesame seeds and
serve at once.

NUTRITION PER SERVE
*Protein 10 g; Fat 15 g;
Carbohydrate 45 g; Dietary
Fibre 6 g; Cholesterol 7 mg;
1580 kJ (375 cal)*

*Warm Green Salad on Noodle Baskets*

# Thai Prawns with Coconut Noodles

*Preparation time:*
*25 minutes*
*Total cooking time:*
*7 minutes*
*Serves 4*

375 g (12 oz) green
  beans, sliced
3/4 cup (185 ml/6 fl oz)
  coconut cream
2 teaspoons finely
  grated lime rind
3 tablespoons oil
300 g (10 oz) instant
  noodles
1 tablespoon finely
  chopped lemon grass
4 spring onions, sliced
750 g (1¹/2 lb) raw
  prawns, peeled and
  deveined
2 tablespoons chopped
  fresh coriander
1–2 tablespoons sweet
  chilli sauce
2 tablespoons lime juice
2 tablespoons fish sauce

1. Boil the beans for
1 minute. Drain, rinse
under cold water, drain
again and set aside.
2. Combine the coconut
cream, lime rind and
1 tablespoon of the oil;
mix well and set aside.
3. Cook the noodles in
plenty of salted boiling
water for 2 minutes, or
until tender. Drain, then
add to a pan with the

coconut cream mixture;
toss gently to combine.
Cover and keep warm.
4. Heat the remaining
oil in a wok and stir-fry
the lemon grass, spring
onion, prawns and
beans over high heat
until the prawns just
turn pink. Toss in the
remaining ingredients,
divide the noodles
between bowls and
spoon the prawns on
top. Serve immediately.

NUTRITION PER SERVE
*Protein 50 g; Fat 40 g;*
*Carbohydrate 55 g; Dietary*
*Fibre 4 g; Cholesterol*
*280 mg; 3265 kJ (775 cal)*

# Peking Hot Spiced Noodles

*Preparation time:*
  *20 minutes*
*Total cooking time:*
  *15 minutes*
*Serves 4*

2 tablespoons oil
3 cloves garlic, chopped
350 g (11 oz) pork
  mince
1¹/2 tablespoons hot
  soy bean paste
2 celery sticks, sliced
1 red capsicum, sliced
1 tablespoon soy sauce
1 tablespoon sesame oil
450 g (14 oz) Hokkien
  noodles, separated
70 g (2¹/4 oz) snow
  peas, halved

1. Place the oil in a
wok over high heat.
When the oil is very
hot, brown the garlic
and pork mince for
4 minutes, breaking up
any lumps—ensure the
wok is very hot or the
meat will 'weep' and
become watery.
2. Reduce the heat to
low, add the hot soy
bean paste and simmer
for 3 minutes. Add the
celery, capsicum, soy
sauce, sesame oil, and
season with a pinch of
salt, white pepper and
sugar. Cover and simmer
for about 3 minutes, or
until the vegetables are
just tender. Keep covered
and set aside.
3. Place the noodles in
a large pan with about
3 tablespoons water.
Cook over medium heat
for 3 minutes, tossing
now and then, or until
plump and hot. Place
the snow peas on top;
cover and steam for
1 minute, adding a little
more water if needed.
4. Remove the snow
peas from the pan and
divide the hot noodles
between serving bowls,
shaking off any excess
water. Top with the
pork and vegetable
mixture and scatter
the snow peas over
the top. Serve at once.

NUTRITION PER SERVE
*Protein 25 g; Fat 25 g;*
*Carbohydrate 30 g; Dietary*
*Fibre 4 g; Cholesterol*
*50 mg; 1915 kJ (455 cal)*

*Thai Prawns with Coconut Noodles (top)*
*and Peking Hot Spiced Noodles*

## Soba Noodle and Chicken Surprise

*Preparation time:*
25 minutes
*Total cooking time:*
45 minutes
*Serves 4*

*1/3 cup (80 ml/2³/4 fl oz)
olive oil
4 slender eggplants,
sliced
1/2 small onion, sliced
into thin strips
1 red capsicum, sliced
2–3 teaspoons ground
cumin
1/2 teaspoon cayenne
pepper
350 g (11¹/4 oz) chicken
thigh fillets, cut into
1 cm (1/2 inch) slices
30 g (1 oz) butter
1 tablespoon lemon juice
1 tablespoon mirin or
dry sherry
200 g (6¹/2 oz) dried
green tea soba noodles
or dried soba noodles
1 tablespoon chopped
fresh parsley*

**1.** In a large pan, heat
3 tablespoons of the oil,
then fry the eggplant
slices over high heat
for about 3 minutes
on each side, or until
golden. Drain, season
to taste and transfer
to a bowl.
**2.** Fry the onion and
capsicum over low heat
for about 5 minutes, or
until softened. Add to
the eggplant.

**3.** Combine the cumin
and cayenne; roll the
chicken in the mixture
to coat. Heat the butter
and remaining oil over
low heat and brown the
chicken for 5–6 minutes.
**4.** Increase the heat to
high. Add the lemon
juice and mirin, and
cook to reduce by half.
Season to taste, remove
from the heat and toss
the chicken through the
vegetables, reserving
the pan juices. Preheat
the oven to moderate
180°C (350°F/Gas 4).
**5.** Cook the noodles in
plenty of boiling salted
water for 5 minutes, or
until tender. Rinse under
warm water and drain.
**6.** Divide the noodles
into 4 portions and
place each on separate
squares of non-stick
baking paper, 30 cm
(12 inches) wide. Fold
up the sides, spoon in
the chicken mixture,
drizzle with pan juices
and sprinkle with the
parsley. Fold up into
parcels, secure tightly,
place on a baking tray
and bake for about
15 minutes. Serve each
parcel on an individual
plate, to be opened at
the table.

NUTRITION PER SERVE
*Protein 25 g; Fat 30 g;
Carbohydrate 45 g; Dietary
Fibre 4 g; Cholesterol
80 mg; 2290 kJ (545 cal)*

## Prawn and Lemon Egg Noodles

*Preparation time:*
15 minutes
*Total cooking time:*
5 minutes
*Serves 4*

*3 tablespoons olive oil
1 clove garlic, crushed
4 spring onions, sliced
750 g (1¹/2 lb) raw
prawns, peeled and
deveined
500 g (1 lb) fresh egg
noodles, cooked and
drained
1 cup (30 g/1 oz) fresh
coriander leaves
1 cup (155 g/5 oz)
frozen peas, cooked
3 tablespoons finely
chopped preserved
lemon
1–2 teaspoons harissa*

**1.** Heat the oil in a
wok or large pan over
high heat. When hot,
add the garlic, spring
onion and prawns;
stir-fry just until the
prawns change colour.
**2.** Add the cooked egg
noodles and remaining
ingredients and stir-fry
until the noodles are
hot. Serve at once.

NUTRITION PER SERVE
*Protein 50 g; Fat 15 g;
Carbohydrate 35 g; Dietary
Fibre 5 g; Cholesterol
280 mg; 2025 kJ (480 cal)*

*Soba Noodle and Chicken Surprise (top)
with Prawn and Lemon Egg Noodles*

# Beef Pho

*Preparation time:*
  15 minutes +
  15 minutes soaking
*Total cooking time:*
  5 minutes
*Serves 4*

225 g (7 oz) dried
  flat rice noodles
1/2 onion, finely sliced
juice of 1 lime
100 g (3$^1$/4 oz) rump
  steak, partially frozen
1.5 litres beef stock
1/3 cup (20 g/$^3$/4 oz)
  chopped fresh
  coriander
1/3 cup (20 g/$^3$/4 oz)
  chopped fresh mint
4 leaves Chinese
  cabbage, finely
  shredded
1 small red chilli, finely
  sliced
1/3 cup (80 ml/2$^3$/4 fl oz)
  fish sauce
lime wedges, to serve

**1.** Soak the noodles in
warm water for about
10 minutes, or until
soft. Soak the onion
in the lime juice.
**2.** Cut the steak across
the grain into strips
2 mm ($^1$/8 inch) thick.
Cover and refrigerate.
**3.** Drain the noodles and
divide between serving
bowls. Heat the stock
to boiling point, reduce
the heat, and leave to
gently simmer.

**4.** Layer the coriander,
mint, Chinese cabbage,
chilli and onion over the
noodles and arrange
the meat on top.
**5.** Pour the boiling
stock over the meat
and noodles to cook
the meat and release
the flavours in the
onion, chilli and herbs.
Add a tablespoon of
fish sauce to each bowl
and serve immediately,
with lime wedges to
squeeze over the top.

**Note:** Chinese cabbage
looks like a white cos
lettuce. It is sometimes
sold in supermarkets,
but if you have trouble
finding any, lettuce may
be used instead.

NUTRITION PER SERVE
*Protein 10 g; Fat 1 g;
Carbohydrate 50 g; Dietary
Fibre 2 g; Cholesterol
15 mg; 1125 kJ (265 cal)*

# Chicken Chow Mein

*Preparation time:*
  25 minutes
*Total cooking time:*
  30 minutes
*Serves 4–6*

*Sauce*
2 teaspoons cornflour
1/2 cup (125 ml/4 fl oz)
  chicken stock
3 tablespoons hoisin
  sauce

375 g (12 oz) dried
  fine egg noodles
3 teaspoons sesame oil
3 tablespoons hoisin
  sauce
oil, for cooking
1 clove garlic, crushed
1 teaspoon grated ginger
1 onion, cut in wedges
500 g (1 lb) chicken
  thigh fillets, cut into
  2 cm ($^3$/4 inch) cubes
1 red capsicum, sliced
1 green capsicum, sliced
12 leaves Chinese
  broccoli, chopped

**1.** Combine the sauce
ingredients and set aside.
**2.** Boil the noodles for
6–8 minutes, or until
tender. Drain well, mix
in the sesame oil and
hoisin sauce; set aside.
**3.** Heat 2 tablespoons
of oil in a wok. Fry the
noodles over medium
heat for 10 minutes, or
until crispy. Drain and
keep warm.
**4.** Heat some more oil
and fry the garlic, ginger
and onion for 2 minutes.
Add the chicken; stir-fry
in batches until tender.
Add the capsicum, cook
for 2 minutes, add the
sauce and stir until thick.
**5.** Add the broccoli and
cook until just wilted.
Slide the noodles onto a
large serving plate, then
spoon the chicken and
vegetables over the top.

NUTRITION PER SERVE
*Protein 25 g; Fat 15 g;
Carbohydrate 55 g; Dietary
Fibre 5 g; Cholesterol
70 mg; 1925 kJ (460 cal)*

*Beef Pho (top) with Chicken Chow Mein*

# Hokkien Noodles with Pesto Beef

*Preparation time:*
40 minutes +
2 hours marinating
*Total cooking time:*
20–25 minutes
*Serves 4*

500 g (1 lb) rump
 steak, partially frozen
3 tablespoons lime juice
1 teaspoon sesame oil
2 red onions, sliced
2 teaspoons olive oil
450 g (14 oz) Hokkien
 noodles
2 teaspoons sugar
extra coriander and red
 onion slices, to garnish

**Coriander Pesto**
2 small red chillies
90 g (3 oz) bunch of
 coriander, roots intact
6 candlenuts, roasted
4 cloves garlic
4 cm (1¹/2 inch) piece
 fresh ginger, peeled
¹/2 cup (125 ml/4fl oz)
 olive oil

**1.** Cut the beef into thin strips across the grain. Set aside in a bowl.
**2.** To make the coriander pesto, roughly chop the chillies, coriander and candlenuts, and finely chop the garlic and ginger. Place in a food processor and process until finely chopped. With the motor still running, slowly add the olive oil to make a paste.
**3.** Add the pesto to the beef with plenty of salt and cracked pepper, add a tablespoon of the lime juice and toss well. Cover and refrigerate for at least 2 hours.
**4.** Heat the sesame oil in a wok and stir-fry the onions over medium heat for 3–4 minutes. Remove and set aside.
**5.** Heat the olive oil and stir-fry the beef in batches over high heat for 3–4 minutes: don't overcrowd the wok, or the meat will stew. Toss

constantly, pushing the meat to the sides of the wok where the heat is. Remove and set aside.
**6.** Gently separate the noodles and add to the wok with 2 tablespoons water, then stir-fry over medium heat until just softened. Cover and steam for 3–4 minutes, adding a little water if the noodles stick.
**7.** Add the onions, beef and 1 tablespoon lime juice; toss quickly for 2 minutes. Add the sugar and remaining lime juice and toss again. Garnish with coriander and sliced red onion and serve at once.

NUTRITION PER SERVE
*Protein 35 g; Fat 40 g; Carbohydrate 35 g; Dietary Fibre 5 g; Cholesterol 85 mg; 2725 kJ (650 cal)*

**Note:** Candlenuts should not be eaten raw. Macadamia nuts can be substituted.

*Hokkien Noodles with Pesto Beef*

*1 Using a sharp knife, thinly slice the partially frozen beef against the grain.*

*2 Roughly chop the bunch of coriander, including the stalks and roots.*

3 With your fingers, gently separate the Hokkien noodles for easier cooking.

4 Cover and steam the softened noodles for 3–4 minutes.

# Roasted Peanut and Noodle Salad

*Preparation time:*
20 minutes +
3 hours refrigeration
*Total cooking time:*
12 minutes
*Serves 4*

250 g (8 oz) dried
 egg noodles
2 teaspoons chilli oil
*1/3 cup (80 ml/2³/4 fl oz)
 rice wine*
*1/3 cup (80 ml/2³/4 fl oz)
 light soy sauce*
2 tablespoons peanut
 oil
1 red capsicum, finely
 diced
*1/2 cup (15 g/¹/2 oz)
 fresh coriander leaves*
*3/4 cup (120 g/4 oz)
 roasted peanuts*

1. Cook the noodles in plenty of boiling salted water for 6–8 minutes, or until tender. Drain, rinse under cold water and drain again.
2. Place in a glass bowl and add the chilli oil, rice wine, soy sauce and half the peanut oil. Toss well; cover and refrigerate for 3 hours.
3. Heat the remaining oil over high heat and stir-fry the capsicum for about 3 minutes, or until lightly cooked. Set aside to cool.

4. Toss the coriander leaves, roasted peanuts and diced capsicum through the noodles until well combined. Spoon onto serving dishes and serve at room temperature.

NUTRITION PER SERVE
*Protein 15 g; Fat 30 g; Carbohydrate 50 g; Dietary Fibre 4 g; Cholesterol 10 mg; 2300 kJ (545 cal)*

# Prawn Ball and Noodle Nests

*Preparation time:*
30 minutes
*Total cooking time:*
25 minutes
*Serves 4*

500 g (1 lb) Hokkien
 noodles, gently pulled
 apart
125 g (4 oz) small snow
 peas, trimmed
500 g (1 lb) raw prawns,
 peeled and deveined
3 cm (1¹/4 inch) piece
 fresh ginger, grated
*1/4 cup (30 g/1 oz)
 cornflour*
1 tablespoon Chinese
 cooking wine
2 cups (500 ml/16 fl oz)
 oil, for deep-frying
2 tablespoons oyster
 sauce
2 tablespoons chicken
 stock
1 tablespoon soy sauce

1. Soak the noodles in hot water for 5 minutes, then drain and place in a colander over a pot of boiling water. Place the snow peas on top to lightly steam them; cover and set aside.
2. Place the prawns, grated ginger, cornflour and Chinese rice wine in a food processor. Season the mixture well, then process until finely chopped and well combined, taking care not to overwork the mixture or it will be too sticky.
3. Place the oil in a wok over medium heat. Shape the prawn mixture into 16 small balls, using wet hands if the mixture gets too soft. Toss the prawn balls around in the oil, in batches, for about 2 minutes each, or until golden. Drain on paper towels and keep warm.
4. Combine the oyster sauce, stock and soy sauce in a small pan and gently bring to the boil, stirring.
5. Transfer the noodles to serving plates and swirl them into 'nests'. Divide the snow peas among the nests and place the prawn balls on top. Drizzle with the sauce and serve at once.

NUTRITION PER SERVE
*Protein 30 g; Fat 20 g; Carbohydrate 40 g; Dietary Fibre 3 g; Cholesterol 185 mg; 2020 kJ (480 cal)*

*Roasted Peanut and Noodle Salad (top)
with Prawn Ball and Noodle Nests*

### BOK CHOY
Also known as Chinese chard or Chinese white cabbage, it has a slightly mustardy taste. Baby bok choy leaves are used whole; cut larger ones in half.

### CANDLENUTS
Large, waxy nuts similar to macadamias. They cannot be eaten raw, but are roasted and ground to enrich sauces. Macadamias can be substituted.

### CHINESE BROCCOLI
A crisp vegetable with dark green leaves and small flowers. The stem is most favoured. It needs only minimal cooking to retain its texture and colour.

### CHINESE COOKING WINE (SHAOSING)
A fermented rice wine. In taste and colour it resembles dry sherry—a good substitute if needed. It is not to be confused with rice wine vinegar.

### DRIED SEAWEED
Nori is the most common variety, sold in sheets or soft shreds, either plain or roasted. Quick toasting over a naked flame gives a fresh, nutty flavour.

### GALANGAL
Related to ginger, this pinkish root has a peppery flavour. Take care when using as it can stain. Dried galangal should be soaked before use.

### GARAM MASALA
A spice blend, often containing cinnamon, cumin, pepper, cloves, cardamom and nutmeg. It can be bought prepacked, but is best freshly made.

### HOT SOY BEAN PASTE
Also called chilli bean paste, and used in Korean cooking, the paste is made from chilli, soy beans, garlic and flavourings. It can be extremely hot!

### KAFFIR LIME LEAVES
These impart a superb fragrance to curries and soups. Fresh leaves are best, and freeze well in airtight bags. Regular lime leaves cannot be substituted.

### KECAP MANIS
This very thick, sweet soy sauce features widely in Indonesian and Malaysian cooking. It is used in sauces for satays, or as a seasoning.

## LEMON GRASS
An aromatic herb, best used fresh. Trim the base, remove the tough outer layers and finely chop the interior. If using dried, soak for half an hour first.

## MIRIN
A mild, low-alcohol form of sake (a Japanese drinking wine made from rice). Mirin, a cooking wine, adds sweetness to sauces, grills and glazes.

## PALM SUGAR
A rich, aromatic sugar sold in blocks or jars, and ranging in colour from pale gold to dark brown. Soft brown sugar can be used instead.

## RICE PAPER WRAPPERS
Clear, flat and brittle, these thin rounds become pliable when brushed with water. They are used to enclose savoury or sweet fillings.

## SAMBAL OELEK
A sambal is a relish. Sambal oelek is a hot sambal made from chillies, salt and vinegar, usually with the chilli seeds left in.

## SHIITAKE MUSHROOMS
These are available fresh or dried. If using dried, soak before use and discard the woody stems. Use the soaking water as a stock or flavouring.

## SHRIMP PASTE
A very pungent paste made from fermented shrimps, often sold in a block. It is always cooked before eating. Store in an airtight container.

## THAI BASIL
Valued by Asian cooks for its aroma, the herb has a purple stem and serrated green and purple leaves. The leaves are added at the end of cooking.

## TONKATSU SAUCE
A tasty, barbecue-style sauce made with apples, tomatoes, Japanese Worcestershire-type sauce and mustard. Barbecue sauce can be used instead.

## VIETNAMESE MINT
Also known as laksa leaf or Cambodian mint, this sharp-tasting herb is not a true mint. It is eaten raw in salads, or used as a garnish.

# Index